Healthy
Passwords

By Ken S. Klein

Sustainable Alternatives, LLC
332 Renie Ln
Ligonier, PA 15658

Visit us on the web at
www.HealthyPasswords.com

Report errors to
errata@HealthyPasswords.com

ISBN 10 -   0615456855
ISBN 13 – 9780615456850

First Edition

Trademarks

Many of the designations used by manufacturers and sellers to distinguish their products are claimed as trademarks. Where those designations appear in this book, and Sustainable Alternatives, LLC was aware of a trademark claim, the designations appear as requested by the owner of the trademark. All other product names and services identified throughout this book are used in editorial fashion only and for the benefit of such companies with no intention of infringement of the trademark. No such use, or the use of any trade name, is intended to convey endorsement or other affiliation with this book.

About this Book

Each page of this book is meant to teach a lesson using real world examples that nearly any age group can understand. This book will:

- Quickly teach important lessons.
- Use common sense examples.
- Use a format conducive to bathroom or bus-stop learning.
- Fit nicely into a purse, briefcase or large pocket.
- Use real-world examples.
- Help the environment by reducing unnecessary paper use.

This book is made for people who would rather focus on learning how to create and use strong passwords than dissecting large technical security guides.

This book describes basic security principals that do not change as fast as hardware and software. Because of this, any references to specific manufacturer hardware or software is covered in the books companion website at healthypasswords.com.

Table of Contents

Preface

Our society has only been using computers widely for the past few decades. Human DNA is not imprinted with innate codes guiding us to pick proper passwords.

Password style can only be learned, but no one in our society seems to be teaching the subject. Kids start using passwords at a young age, yet schools rarely devote any time to them. If they do, it may be at the discretion of the teacher and limited to their understanding of the subject.

The few password guides around are either one page long or mostly geared towards the information technology (IT) professional.

Publishers may shy away from password books because the subject is rather small and filling an entire full-length technical book requires much more subject matter than just passwords.

This book teaches healthy password use by using common examples from everyday life that most anyone can relate to.

This guide is meant to teach grandparents, parents and children how to create and use their own strong, memorable passwords.

Healthy Password Rules:

This book provides a system to create memorable, strong passwords.

1. Quality Ingredients Make Healthy Passwords.

   Use strong passwords

2. Choose your dining locations carefully.

   Have a special place for finances

3. Wash your hands before you eat.

   Computer viruses and malware are germs.

Food is used as a metaphor to teach basic password, computer and network security.

Why are Passwords Important?

Stealing passwords for money is understandable, but why does anyone want your family pictures, birthdays or other information? Most people don't care about those things. But increasingly there are incidents where criminals "mine" personal data from sites solely for the purpose of planning a physical crime.

Sites like Facebook™ provide robust security settings. When your password is stolen, all of those settings are bypassed.

Passwords seem like a nuisance at many sites. Everyone understands their benefit at sites holding your financial data. The reason so many sites require passwords is to retrieve your settings. These may be insignificant items like the screen layout, colors, or the last time you posted information. It's how the site knows who you are. In technical terms the process is called authentication.

When account access is gained by breaking your password, the perpetrator is impersonating you. They may:

1. Purchase things using your saved checkout settings.

2. Look at details which are private.

3. Change details to embarrass or slander you.

4. Falsely broadcast messages to your co-workers, customers, friends and family.

5. Transfer funds from your accounts.

6. Download your personal documents and files.

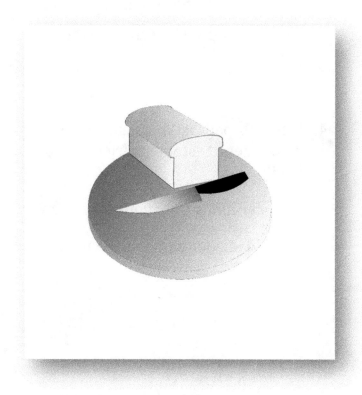

Rule 1 – Quality Ingredients Make Healthy Passwords

Learn to assemble your own ingredient list

Anyone can build a strong password. Remembering it is hard.

Easily remembering passwords requires a system.

A good system needs to:

1. Be made of smaller re-usable parts.
2. Make it easy to re-order parts.
3. Only require memorization of short phrases.
4. Easily accommodate long password lengths.

Fact *A character is any letter, number, or punctuation mark.*

Strong Characters Make Strong Passwords

Password strength is determined by:

1. Overall password length.

   Longer usually means better. If you choose your characters wisely, you can make stronger passwords using fewer characters.

2. Combination of characters used.

   Avoid repeating characters, always mix letters, numbers and symbols. Always vary upper and lower case.

3. It should not be a dictionary word.

   Dictionary words should be avoided. One of the first things cracking programs do is try "password". Shortly after they try "drowssap" (password spelled backward).

4. Avoid using numeric or alphabetical series such as:

   - abcdef
   - 123456
   - 987654

   Unfortunately, the most common passwords used by people is 123456.

Fact *Because your bank revokes your account after three tries, don't assume cracking programs will hit the same limitation. Automated programs don't actually crack the password using the real site. They use breadcrumbs (encrypted copies of the password left behind on your computer or stolen from the site). They try millions of variations very quickly.*

5. Avoid using character substitution with dictionary words. Character substitution swaps symbols or numbers with letters. For example S becomes $ or I becomes 1.

   This looks like a good password, but it's not:

   P@$$w0rd

   Cracking programs try character substitutions and will quickly crack this password.

Kids and Pets: The worst passwords

One of the most common passwords is using a child or pet name. This is the first thing someone who knows you will try when breaking your password.

If you must use them, then try using first, middle and last initials. For example:

Kids	John Robert Doe
	Jane Sue Doe

Make the password of: `jrdjsd`

Try some spice

Want to spice things up a bit, let us mix case first. Passwords are usually "Case Sensitive", so to a computer, "a" is different than "A". We can start by capitalizing middle initials.

`jRdjSd` is a little better.

If you do not like the uppercase, then let's add a number signifying their birth order. Jane was born before John, so how about adding a two after jrd and a one after jsd?

`jrd2jsd1` is much better.

Whistle While You Cook

Can You Remember Three Blind Mice?

As you will soon see, phrases are a good way to create your passwords. The first letter of each word in the phrase can make up part of your password. The phrase "three blind mice" creates the password "tbm".

A three-letter password is very weak. To strengthen it you can choose a longer phrase, but longer phrases make ingredient re-use across multiple sites tough. Another option is to surround the phrase with two other abbreviations. An easy visual representation is a password sandwich.

The Password Sandwich

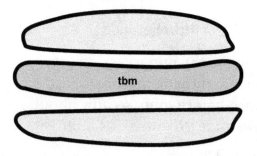

Password = tbm
Strength = Very Weak

Choosing the Bread

You know that whole grain bread is supposed to be better for you than plain white bread.

There are times when plain white bread is sufficient, such as a password to a site that keeps no important data about you.

White Bread Examples:

Birth dates are one of the worst things you can use as a password. To illustrate how the sandwich concept works, we will make a strong password from ingredients as insecure as birthdays.

Birth Month: 04

Birth Day: 13

Birth year: 66

Birth Century: 19

Using two pieces of white bread for our sandwich gives us a slightly better password. Nevertheless, it is still weak.

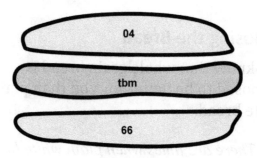

Password = 04tbm66
Strength = Weak

! *If you use personal dates, adopt a policy where you always subtract or add something from the real day. If you choose to always subtract one, then consistently subtract one. Consistency aids memory.*

Whole Wheat Bread Examples:

1. Birth month & day code: a12 (for April 12)

2. Site Abbreviation: @az (At Amazon™)

3. Your favorite personal identification number (PIN) split up.
    Do you have a PIN you have used for your ATM/Debit card? It is definitely not good to use the pin by itself, but pins are normally memorized four digit numbers.
    This is if your PIN does not repeat the same number multiple times. If it does, call your bank to find out how to change it. It should be at least a four digit number having no more than one number repeated.

4. Can you still remember the last four digits of your childhood phone number? Most people still do. (If it is still your parent's phone number, do not use it.)

5. Do you have an identification number memorized? Try the first or last four digits of that number.

6. Expiration dates: These are your own codes that remind you to change your password. Some examples are Q2

(Expires second quarter), or A2 (Expires annually every February).

Getting back to our sandwich, to change our bread from white to whole wheat we can slightly alter our dates to three characters such as a12tbmy66.

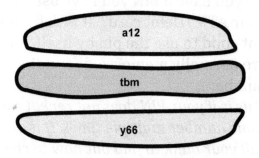

Password = a12tbmy66
Strength = Moderate

> **!** *Security experts will say to never use birthdates' or phone numbers, but if they're split in half and separated by several letters, numbers and special characters, it's OK to use them.*

What About Condiments?

We now have a proper sandwich with bread and a main ingredient, but it is still not strong. Most people like a little ketchup, mayonnaise, mustard or cheese on their sandwich. To strengthen our password further, we can do the same thing by adding special characters.

Special characters enhance our passwords turning a moderate password into a strong password. You only need to rely upon one or two special characters.

Let's add our condiments. We will add a comma and a period.

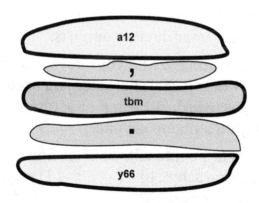

Password = a12,tbm.y66
Strength = Strong

Most English keyboards have over 30 special characters. When selecting special characters, try to use ones that are comfortable for you to type. Some common special characters for passwords are:

Character	Description
_	Underscore
!	Exclamation
@	"AT" Symbol
*	Asterisk
#	Hash

If you will access a site on a device that does not have a keyboard, try using special characters your device supports.

It is frustrating to find your device does not support the special character you used in a great password. A Hash # or asterisk * is usually on a phone keypad.

For kids or people with shorter fingers, special characters like (, . ; : < >{ }) may be easier to type on a standard keyboard.

! *Some sites don't allow special characters in passwords. When they don't, you may need to substitute with numbers and mixed-case less common letters such as xYzQ.*

Add a Little Spice

Our last example was a strong password, but it is still missing one last thing. The difference between an average sandwich and a gourmet sandwich is in the spice.

Adding spice is a matter of changing a letter's case upper or lower).

The best place to mix lowercase and uppercase letters is in the phrase, which should be your main ingredient. If you start each phrase with a capital (uppercase) letter, you will strengthen your password.

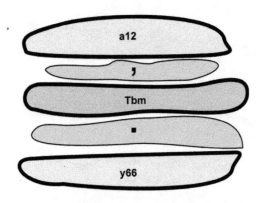

Password = a12,Tbm.y66
Strength = Very Strong

We have completed our first password sandwich. There is no definitive scale for password strength. There are many password strength checkers on the internet. Rather than relying upon a single checker, you should try a few. You will find results vary. *Note to Mac users. OS-X has a nice password strength checker built into the user configuration utilities. See Managing accounts on page 129.*

Password strength checkers are online utilities you can find on websites, which enable you to see your password strength in real-time. A listing of recommended password strength checkers can be found at www.HealthyPasswords.com.

Use caution with on-line password checkers. Only trust known reputable sites using encrypted (HTTPS) connections. See page 141 for more information on HTTPS.

Using three online password checkers, our "a12,Tbm.y66" password was rated as "Strong", "Very Strong" and "Reasonable".

You may be tempted to put this book down now and start making passwords.

At this point you can make one strong password, but creating a good password plan that works well for multiple sites requires more information.

If you start changing passwords without a plan, you will quickly get frustrated and go back to weak passwords.

The First Ingredient List Reviewed

Let us review our first ingredient list. Creating a good ingredient list can enable us to accommodate multiple sites without repeating passwords at any two sites.

a12 is a type of code representing our birth month and date. The real date is 4/13, but it is best not to use a significant date. We subtracted 1 from the date and used "a" instead of "04" or "APR". You can adopt your own strategy. Consistent strategies are memorable.

, (Comma) is a condiment used to connect the top slice of bread with the main ingredient. If you plan to use a mobile phone or device, an asterisk (*) may be a better choice here.

Tbm is our main ingredient. It is a rhythmic phrase known by any child: Three Blind Mice. There can be many variations when creating the main ingredient, as you will soon see. We added spice to Tbm by making the "T" uppercase.

• (Period) is a condiment used to connect the main ingredient with the bottom slice of bread. Notice the period as the last condiment, just as it is when used in a sentence. Like the previous condiment, if you are using it on a mobile device, a hash (#) may be a better choice. (If you look at a phone number pad, the asterisk is to the left and the hash is to the right. This is why we recommend using them in that order.)

y66 Stands for the birth year. It is the bottom slice of bread.

The next section will go into more detail on other ingredient options for stronger passwords.

Characteristics of a Strong Password:

1. Be at least ten characters.

2. Include a mix of lower case and upper case letters.

3. Include at least one number.

4. Include at least one special character.

5. Is not a dictionary word (even spelled backward).

6. Internet searches for your main ingredient should not return any meaningful results.

7. Do not use series like abc or 123 or 321.

8. Avoid character substitution for dictionary words.

Choosing the Fillings

Grilled Cheese is a little less complicated than a Bacon Lettuce & Tomato. What about a club sandwich?

Each ingredient by itself is simple, but when combined in different ways, they make strong passwords.

Choosing Memorable Ingredients

There are many methods to choosing the right ingredients for your sandwich.

1. **Rhythmic Phrases:**

   You have already seen how a rhythmic phrase like "Three Blind Mice" can be the focal point of a memorable password.

   Not all of these will work though. Using "Row Row Row Your Boat", would not be effective, because it repeats R too many times and doesn't add enough variety to the entire phrase. Get creative. You could use r3yb to represent it instead.

2. Songs:

Is there a song that has been in your head for years? Use the first letter of each word.

> Fact *Avoid using popular numbers like 8675309.*

3. Your Favorite Things:

My favorite <BLANK> is <BLANK> You fill in the blanks. How about:

Mfc=Vwb	My favorite car equals Volkswagen Bus
Mff=Lmb	My favorite fish equals Largemouth bass
Msfp=ftq	My second favorite poker equals follow the queen

If you happen to make a word out of your favorite thing, choose a different favorite. My favorite poker game is Texas Hold Em, but that made the word the, which is a dictionary word, so I used my second favorite game.

4. Sports Teams:

How about using sports acronyms such as NYY for New York Yankees or NYJ for New York Jets.

5. Airport Codes:

Frequent fliers may like to use their favorite airport codes. How about DET (Detroit) or ORD. (Chicago O'Hare)

6. Your Own Essence Phrase:

Vsg	Very smart girl
Wbd	Worlds best dad
Lam	Lean and mean

7. Religious Passages

Are you good at sighting passages from your favorite holy text? Use your favorite ones. Just be sure to not use complete specific passage identifiers, since they are equivalent to dictionary words.

Different Restaurants Different Dishes

When choosing ingredients, one must consider the occasion.

You wouldn't serve TV dinners for a holiday. You need different passwords for different site types.

Occasions

High-end Restaurants (Strong Passwords)		Financial Sites
		Work Logins
Family Chains (Moderate Passwords)	Sit down	Email
		On-line Shopping Sites
	Buffet	Social Networks
		Computer Logins
Fast Food (Weak Passwords)		Forums and Special Interest Groups

Don't Let Your Sandwich Spoil

Passwords should have expiration dates. The expiration dates will vary by site type.

In this book's last chapter, you will learn to categorize sites by risk levels. The highest risk sites are financial sites. These sites need to have their password change a minimum of every three months (quarterly).

Including expiration dates in your password is a good way to remember to change it. It also adds variety to your password.

In general, passwords will need to change every month, every three months, or every year.

Highest Risk Sites	Change every 1-3 months.
High Risk Sites	Change every 6-12 months
Moderate Risk Sites	Change every 9-12 months

Our previous password was "a12,Tbm.y66". When considering how to integrate the expiration we have two choices: We can add the expiration to the password, or we can swap out an ingredient with the expiration.

Since we are just starting out with strong passwords, let us keep it as short as possible. We will replace the less secure birth year with an expiration date. We will pretend the site we have made this password for is for online banking, and we are going to change it quarterly. Our new password sandwich will be:

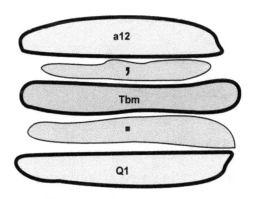

Password = a12,Tbm.Q1
Strength = Strong

Changing the bottom slice of bread from y66 to Q1 added an uppercase letter, but removed a number and shortened our length.

A better approach may be to swap the bottom bread for expiration, but also strengthen the main ingredient. We will strengthen this by combining two phrases. We will combine "Three blind mice" with "See how they run".

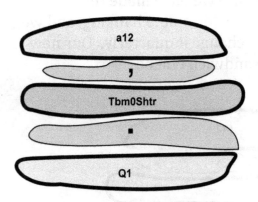

Password = a12,Tbm0Shtr.Q1
Strength = Very Strong

We will also add a little spice by separating the phrases with a zero. This is considered VERY STRONG. In practice, many sites do not allow a fifteen-character password, so research your highest risk sites before making a password this long.

Never Use the Same Password for Multiple Sites.

How can you possibly keep it straight when every site has a different password? Use the same ingredients but change the order or quantities. Incorporating site abbreviations into your passwords works very well for most people.

> *Would you order Lobster at a fast food restaurant? Why would you use your bank password at a needlepoint site?*

Every time you log into a site, you are potentially broadcasting your password.

Some sites treat passwords the way old-fashioned diners treat your order. They take the order quietly from you then yell it back to the kitchen where everyone at the bar can listen.

People run sites. Even if they do not broadcast it, someone who works in the kitchen may read the order. If a dishonest person working at one site decodes your password, they can try using it at other popular sites. By keeping passwords unique by site, you can help to minimize exposure.

Most large reputable sites have solid policies to prevent access to customer password lists. Small sites may not have the resources to implement and enforce such policies.

A good strategy is to have at least two main ingredients on your ingredient list. Use a low quality main ingredient for the small sites and use a high quality main ingredient for reputable sites.

Your low-quality main ingredient could be another phrase, or it could even be made of family initials. A small site having very little personal information is a good candidate for using lower quality passwords.

Sites that keep no more than an email address and some site settings can all use the same password. You may only visit these sites every few months. You need a favorite junk food password, which you will always try first when visiting them. Chances are good that you currently have that one bad password already in use, so you may not need to change anything for these types of sites.

Sample Multi Site Menu

The following table incorporates seven (7) ingredients, which cover all risk-level sites, to create unique passwords. The owner of these passwords needs to know four basic recipes. The variables are in the site identifier and expiration, which are easily memorable variations.

Risk Level	Site	Top Bread	Condiment	Main Ingredient	Condiment	Bottom Bread
Highest	First Bank	Fb	@	TbmShtr	!	Q1
Highest	Second Bank	Sb	@	TbmShtr	!	Q2
High	Amazon™	az	@	Shtr		A2
High	Overstock™	os	@	Shtr		A2
Moderate	Twitter™	tw	@	Tbm		A2
Moderate	Facebook™	fb	@	Tbm		A1
Low	Knitters Anonymous			Jrdjsd		
Low	Cats Best Friend			Jrdjsd		

The banks, our highest risk sites, use five ingredients.

First Bank	fb	@	TbmShtr	!	Q1
Second Bank	sb	@	TbmShtr	!	Q2

1. They have a top slice with the site identifier.

2. They have a condiment, the @ symbol. *As a memory device the AT symbol represents "at this site".*

3. They have a double phrase main ingredient. (Three Blind Mice See How They Run). The first letter of each phrase is capitalized this is consistent for all our passwords.

4. They have an exclamation condiment after the main ingredient. *As a memory device exclamation is like expiration.*

5. They have an expiration date by quarter.

A good shorthand for highest risk sites is:

```
ss at 3br1 3br2 ex Qx
```

Note: 3br stands for "3 Blind Rodents (AKA Mice) The trailing 1 or 2 represents the first or second part of the phrases.

Shopping sites, our high risk sites, use just four ingredients.

Amazon™	az	@	Shtr		A2
Overstock™	os	@	Shtr		A2

1. They have a top slice that is also a site identifier,

2. They have a condiment, which is also the @ symbol.

3. They only use the second part of the three blind mice phrase (See How They Run).

4. They don't have a condiment for expiration

5. They have an expiration code, which is annual rather than quarterly. They both expire in February.

A good shorthand for high risk sites is:

```
ss at 3br2 Ax
```

Social Networking sites, our moderate risk sites, use just four of the sandwich parts.

Twitter™	tw	@	Tbm		A2
Facebook™	fb	@	Tbm		A1

Note: If you have a large following on social networking sites, such as celebrities or politicians, then Social Networking sites should be considered highest risk.

1. They have a top slice, which is also a site identifier.

2. They have a condiment, which is also the @ symbol.

3. They have only the first part of the three blind mice main ingredient.

4. They have an expiration code, which is also annual. They expire in February and January.

A good shorthand for moderate risk sites is:

```
ss at 3br2 Ax
```

Low risk sites, use just one of the sandwich parts.

Knitters Anonymous			Jrdjsd		
Cats Best Friend			Jrdjsd		

1. They use the junk food main ingredient of our kids initials.

A good shorthand for the low risk sites is:

K2K1

Note: If you missed "Kids and Pets: The worst passwords" look at page 19.

Your own wallet card menu

If you adopt a format where all sites share the same format by risk level, you can keep a very simple wallet card to use until you get things remembered.

Hgst: ss at 3br1 3br2 ex Qx

Hg: ss at 3br2 Ax

Mod: ss at 3br1 Ax

Low: k2k1

You can even use the back-side of the card to note exceptions.

If someone finds your wallet card, They will not have any idea what it is for. You will only need to remember how sites were classified and some of your shorthand.

Ss=Site Identifier

3br1 = Three Blind Mice

3br2 = See how they run

Ax = Annual Expiration

Qx = Quarterly Expiration

K2 = 2nd Child initials

K1 = 1st Child initials

At = @

Ex = !

This sample site menu is only a quick example of how to make a password plan. See "Your First Menu" on page 91 for a more detailed action-plan .

Summary

1. Strong passwords are at least 10 characters long and contain mixed case letters, numbers and symbols.

2. Strong passwords can be memorable.

3. Break passwords into parts using a simple memory system like the password sandwich.

4. Use phrases to make the main ingredient of your password sandwich.

5. Password strength should match the site need.

6. Do not use the same password for moderate, high, or highest risk sites.

7. Passwords need to expire and change regularly. Building expiration into the password strengthens it acting as a reminder to change it.

8. If you are currently using weak passwords, use this system to create moderate passwords. You can always go to strong passwords later.

Making strong passwords is only half of the battle. Learning to safely use them is just as important.

You can make the best password in the world, but if you use it on a device having a keystroke logger installed, your efforts will be wasted.

Don't start changing passwords yet. At a minimum, you need a plan. The next two chapters teach you how to use the passwords you create. The last chapter teaches you how to create and implement your action plan.

Rule 2 - Choose Your Dining Locations Carefully

Have a Special Place for Finances

You can make a healthy sandwich. Can you safely eat it?

You have learned to wrap your password in bread with condiments, spices and nice healthy fillings. Do you make one, and then run straight to the bathroom to eat it?

Four Star Restaurant, Diner, or Fast Food

The location where your password is used does not necessarily mean the place or computer you use. The way that you log in also matters.

Like choosing a restaurant, you need to choose your location based on the following needs:

Finance

These are things you do such as use financial software, access on-line banking, perform stock trading, or perform other investment or retirement account activities.

Risky Activities

These are things like online games, online pharmacies, adult content, or gambling. Keep in mind that many of these sites are completely safe. You should do research about a site before trusting it. Just because a site was once safe, it may not remain safe. Periodically review the sites you use.

There are third party utilities which regularly test and rate websites. Some of these offer browser plug-ins, which will display the latest site status and test dates right on the browser. For a recent list of third-party software, visit the online reference to this book at www.HealthyPasswords.com

Work

Work is any activity you do on a computer to earn income.

Everything else

This is day-to-day activities like reading email, monitoring news, updating documents, playing games, etc.

I Only Have One Computer!

Most of today's computers (Operating Systems) offer multiple user accounts. Depending on how your system was setup, you may have never seen the login screen.

Computer accounts are how the operating system segregates roles and resources. People may not be asked to login when they turn on their computer. This usually means they are running as an administrator level user. It is like having the access to walk into a restaurant's kitchen and start messing with their equipment.

When it comes to your computer, you want to be like the customer. For normal activities, you only touch your own plate. You can save your own files in your own directory. You can read your own email. You can change your desktop backgrounds and do what you need for your common everyday tasks, but you cannot mess with the inner workings to let germs in.

See Appendix A on page 115 for more information on setting up user accounts.

Microsoft Windows™, Apple OS-X™, and Linux™ all make it easy to setup different user accounts.

> *You need a minimum of two accounts: One for finance and another for everything else[1]. When you want to check your bank account or pay some bills, resist the temptation to not log into that special account. Before you setup the new account, it is best to clean your system if possible. See page 81 for more details.*

High Risk Protection

Risky sites attract germs. If you only have one computer and you cannot prohibit certain activities, at least create a limited rights account for this activity and only let it happen there. *(See Appendix* A – Creating Additional User Accounts *on page 115 for more information on limited rights accounts.)*

When you visit risky sites while logged in as an administrator-level user, you may

---

[1] If you are applying these principals in business, it may be impossible to get two logins. Most enterprises use a single login, which authenticates against a directory service. If you are concerned about security, you should consult your company's appropriate IT manager.

compromise the account. See "Rule 3 - Wash your hands before you eat" on page 81 for more information on this.

> *You can boot from a live-CD to perform high-risk activities. See page 60 for more information.*

Do Not Work Where You Play

If you drive somewhere else from 9-5, and occasionally need to check-in after hours, it is ideal to have a company furnished laptop.

If your position cannot justify that, you need to be especially careful when logging into work from a home computer.

As a consumer, there are protections to get back most of your money when your financial passwords are used, but business accounts do not have the same protections.

If you are one of the people responsible for your business' bank accounts, you need more than just a strong password. Take a look at "Keeping the Sandwich Factory Running" on page 64.

The Ultimate Germ Protection

The best protection for online finance is to use a non-writable operating system. Non-writable operating systems do not change. There is no way for malicious programs to get onto the CD. Every time you turn them on, they revert to their original state.

There are two ways to use a non-writable OS:

1. Live CD
2. Virtual Machine (non-persistent)

Live CD

This is slow and not convenient, but the least expensive and depending on your hardware, possibly the easiest option.

Getting one of these to work is a hit-or-miss proposition. If you are comfortable with burning CDs and DVDs, you can download free Live-CDs. For more information on good live-cd distributions to use, look at www.HealthyPasswords.com. If you are not comfortable, making your own, go to the local bookstore and buy one or two Linux magazines with "Live-CDs" included.

Once you have the CD or DVD, insert it into your computers CD/DVD drive and power

it on. In some cases, the computer may
ignore the CD and just start as it normally
does. If it ignores it, you may have to pull
out your manual or look online to find out
how to configure your computer to boot
from the optical drive. Once your computer
boots up using the live CD, you will have to
make choices. If given the choice to install
the CD, do not do this. Just run it from the
CD.

Virtual Machine

A virtual machine is software that runs a
virtual computer in a window on your
existing computer. For this to work, the
computer running the virtual machine
must be powerful enough to enable the
virtual machine to run. If you have a new
computer, it probably is. If you have an old
computer, it may not be.

Configured properly, a virtual machine can
protect you from many bad things, but the
biggest flaw is that it cannot protect you
from keystroke loggers like a live-CD can.

Virtual machines are not as secure as live-
CDs because keyboard loggers running on
your main system still have the ability to
capture passwords, but that ability is
slightly handicapped.

> *A suggested strategy is to use a live-CD for "good" sites you don't want bad people to get into and to use a virtual machine for "bad" sites where criminals may be lurking, such as adult content, gambling, or international pharmaceutical sites.*

If you use a virtual machine, be sure to change its hard-drive to be "non-persistent" after you get the operating system installed, patched, and working as needed. This will prevent any changes from occurring.

You can also use a virtual machine to run a live-cd image. Virtual machines are an advanced topic. More content is available at HealthyPasswords.com.

What about tablets and net-books?

Tablet and net-book computing has just begun to gain momentum, and the early versions of many tablet operating systems do not allow multiple login accounts or have CD drives to boot live-CDs from.

Some solutions are being created to address this issue. One such idea is to run multiple accounts in the browser itself, which offers a little added protection. Another possible idea is to use remote control software to access a secure desktop account. Until you have a good alternative or tablets mature a bit, you are best to do finances elsewhere.

Keeping the Sandwich Factory Running

Every week some small business or municipality employee logs into their payroll account to discover it has been wiped out. When a business bank account is stolen, banks have limited liability forcing the business to write-off most of the loss. The loss of a small businesses payroll account can force many small businesses into bankruptcy. There are insurance companies willing to write policies against such fraud. If you are a small business owner, it is advisable to research such policies.

> *If you are a person responsible for your company's online bank accounts, you need to take extraordinary precautions.*

Working from home usually occurs in the form of three different methods:

1. Virtual Private Network (VPN)

   This is when you use software to connect to work through your existing home broadband or dial-up connection. When you are connected to work via VPN, it is as if your home computer is on the work network. If your home computer is compromised, attackers have full access to your work resources. Most businesses with dedicated IT departments will have adequate protections in place. Many small businesses do not have the resources and will be more vulnerable.

2. Web Portals

    This is when you navigate your browser to a work website to check email or run utilities. This is generally a safer way to access the work environment, because it only exposes a few resources to your home computer. If you use this type of setup, you can be a little less vigilant.

3. Dial-up Remote Control

    This is when you run a third party utility to dial into a specific computer running emulation software. With the introduction of VPN and Web Portals, this has become very uncommon. You can be less vigilant, since the remote

control software on both ends is
working with each other, which is
relatively safe[2].

Working from the road is another hazard.

1. Free WIFI™ (Worst)

   You must be very careful using any free
   WIFI™. A worst case issue with free
   WIFI™ may be where a criminal sets up
   a wireless access point in an airport or
   near a cafe for the sole purpose of fraud.
   They may act as a middle point,
   capturing everything between your
   computer and the site you are using.
   They may also just attempt to access
   your file system to steal files. Free
   WIFI™ lacks encryption most of the
   time, so everything you do online is
   visible to any interested criminal within
   proximity.

2. Pay per use WIFI™ (Better)

   Pay per use WIFI™ is normally a service
   run by third-party carriers or providers.
   As long as the service uses some form of

---

[2] Open modems on business networks are a different security
risk, which is beyond the control of the average employee.

encryption it will be safer than free WIFI™. In many cases the provider will require you to use their software to connect. If you are not sure that your connection is encrypted, call the companies support number and ask. If it is not, you should not be paying for it. This takes care of the encryption configuration. If a company you have never heard of is running the service, you should be a little sceptical and not connect to any financial sites or sensitive sites. *See appendix B on page 135 to learn about WIFI™ encryption.*

3. Cellular Card (Best)

All major cellular carriers now offer data services for internet access via their cellular network. These services normally require a USB device or a card that goes into your laptop (PCMCIA). In some cases, you may connect your cell phone to the computer via USB (A process called tethering).

It has also become common to see phones that become WiFi access points themself. If your phone does this, be

sure that it's configured to use WPA2 or
WPA.

> *Cellular cards are the safest
> way to connect while travelling.
> Be certain it is connecting via
> cellular and not using WIFI
> when available.*

4. Hotel Internet (Hit or Miss)

Hotel internet comes in two flavors
(WIFI™ and wired). Either flavor is like
a hybrid between Free WIFI™ and pay
per use WIFI™. It is normally restricted
to hotel guests only. This restriction by
itself may provide adequate encryption
on the wireless side, but even then it
could be unsecure later on. If the hotel
offers wireless in the lobbies and wired
in the rooms and the access points for
wireless just connect to the same
segment every room is on, then anyone
in a room with a little skill and proper
software can see everything everyone
else is doing. Even the one's who are on
a secure wireless, because the access
point decrypts it then send it over the
wired connection unencrypted.

The only safe option in a hotel is to use a VPN connection. This creates a secure tunnel between your computer and the VPN hardware at the other end.

You may already have a VPN client to connect to work, if you do, always connect to VPN before doing anything while travelling. You should also consider company policy of resource use. When travelling on company business, it may be acceptable. If you do not have access to a work VPN, you can purchase a subscription to a personal VPN service.

Do an internet search for personal VPN and you will find there are dozens. For a complete list, look at this books reference at healthypasswords.com.

If you find yourself forced to use a questionable connection, try using only encrypted websites. Encrypted website URLs begin with HTTPS instead of HTTP. You may be able to just add an 'S' to your website's URL. Some sites offer encrypted services without defaulting to them.

Keeping the Kitchen Clean

Infrastructure is the equipment installed in your home enabling computers and devices to access each other and the outside world.

> *If you use a dial-up modem in a single computer, you don't need to worry about this section.*

Point of Entry

Routers are the most important infrastructure equipment in your home. They are usually a small box connected to your phone or cable television line. They connect your home to the internet. Routers are also the way others can get into your home network.

Every router sold comes with default passwords. Most manufacturers have one or two default passwords for their equipment.

> *At a minimum, you should change your router's default passwords.*

The most common user-name and password for home routers is "admin" for both the username and password. A quick internet search will give you a listing of default admin passwords by router manufacturer.

If you leave your router password at the default and your router allows remote configuration, anyone can connect to your router and reconfigure it.

Most routers do not have remote configuration enabled, but as routers age, vulnerabilities surface allowing backdoors for intruders to get in even when remote configuration is disabled.

A criminal with admin access to your router can change the "DNS" server directing your traffic to their fake server. When you then type mybank.com into your browser, their DNS server directs you to their own fake bank site, where they steal your password then promptly login to the real site to transfer out your money.

Over the past few years, there has been a Windows virus known as the Google virus, which installs itself on windows computers in a very hidden way, so that anti-virus programs have a difficult time detecting it. This virus simply changes your google search results to direct you to fake pages.

> *Did you wonder why your bank displays a photo you previously selected after keying your user name? Fake sites are the very reason. If your bank doesn't offer this, look for a new bank that does.*

If you have a single computer connected to a home broadband router, your job will be relatively easy. You will just need to ensure your computer and router are protected. You can do many advanced things to lock-down your router. You may need the help of a local professional.

If you have a router with wireless capabilities enabled you are providing two ways into your house. Intruders can enter through the wire (phone or cable tv line coming into the router), or intruders within proximity (usually limited to people next door or driving by) can connect to your wireless network. Once connected, they may have access to any vulnerable computers or devices in your home.

It is becoming very common for innocent homeowners to go through embarrassing ordeals because they failed to lock down their wireless access point or router.

Learn the best ways to lock-down your wireless network in Appendix B – WiFi™ on page 135.

Targets

Now that you know how intruders get in, the next step is to find vulnerabilities.

In recent years, there has been a proliferation of network enabled appliances. A few network enabled appliances include:

Commonly Enabled Devices

- Computers
- Printers
- Network Storage Devices
- Security Systems/Cameras
- Game Consoles
- Smart Phones, PDAs, Internet Tablets
- DVRs
- Baby Monitors
- Some Televisions
- Streaming Appliances (For Internet TV)
- Blue Ray / DVD Players

If you have these devices, you should determine your risks.

Personal Safety

The only things you cannot replace are people. Any device allowing an intruder to enter your home physically needs to have top priority.

If you have one or more security cameras at home, you already know this. The same cameras that help you monitor your home can monitor you. If your security cameras are accessible from outside the home, be sure to configure them correctly and choose strong passwords. The most important first step is to change the default manufacturer passwords. If you are unsure of their capabilities, seek the advice of a professional.

An even bigger risk in personal safety may be the things you broadcast. If you feel compelled to broadcast every move you make via social networking or messaging sites, do not be surprised if someone visits your home after you tell everyone that you are having a wonderful weekend away. Likewise, you should not tell the world that just part of your family is away and a few vulnerable ones are home alone.

Device Safety

There is not much to gain by hacking into a television, DVR or blue-ray™ player. If however you have a Network attached storage device to store or backup your data, you should be concerned. It is common to back up tax returns, credit reports, and bank statements just to mention a few types of files you may backup.

Bandwidth Preservation

Wireless routers need some level of rudimentary encryption and a password setup to prevent unwanted users from using your internet. If you live in a rural area where the closest neighbor lives a mile away, you do not need to worry much. If however, you live in an apartment complex or even a tight suburban development, you may find your network is slow because the neighbors are getting free internet from you. It is not too difficult to break a wireless routers security. There are programs, which can figure this out quickly. If you setup a strong password, most people will try for an easier target.

Everyone needs to take wireless security seriously. It is becoming more common to hear of innocent people being falsely arrested because others used their access point for criminal activities. Take a look at Appendix B on page 135 for more information on WiFi™. There is also more information on wireless security at www.heathypasswords.com

Summary

1. Different sites require different password strengths.

2. Segregate your online activities using different accounts.

3. Never mix finance with other high-risk activities.

4. Change the default passwords on your home router.

5. If you use home equipment to access work networks, be careful.

6. Evaluate your home network devices for safety.

Rule 3: Wash Your Hands Before You Eat

Computer Viruses and Malware are Germs

Clean Environments Reduce Germs

The best password in the world will not protect you, if it has been used it on a compromised machine.

You need a clean environment. Think of computer viruses and malware as germs that want to steal your valuables.

Clean your machine

1. Buy the latest operating system for your computer and have it installed clean (not upgraded). (You may need some help)

2. Do a clean install of your operating system. Instead of buying a new operating system, just start over with the existing one. Install a fresh copy using your system restore CDs to wipe out the existing copy. (If your computer is not old, the seller may offer phone support to help re-install it.)

3. If your computer is so old that it will not run the latest operating system, try to buy a new computer running the latest operating system.

> ! *Presently Windows XP™ is the most attacked operating system in the world. If you are running it, you should consider upgrading to the latest version. If you don't want to upgrade, you should clean your machine and be sure to update it so that every security update available is applied.*

Keeping your Machine Clean

1. Have multiple accounts (Logins) created on your machine, which have limited rights.

   Use one account for your own everyday use.

   Have a separate account for Finances only. Only use this account for finances.

2. Do not let kids use this machine!

   Kids have a way of attracting computer viruses. If you cannot afford to give kids their own machine, at least setup a separate account with very limited rights.

3. Install a good third party virus protection suite.

4. Keep the computer up to date with all patches and upgrades.

5. Don't use promiscuous USB drives.

   Viruses and Malware are commonly spread from USB drives.

Never plug a USB drive (also known as flash drive) that's been used on other machines while logged in as one of your secure accounts.

Switch to the limited rights account to plug in the drive, and be sure to scan it using your virus software.

Maintain Your Cookware

One of the biggest threats to your computer is old programs. Antivirus products ignore many of the installed programs running on your computer. Attackers have found that targeting these older programs is the easiest way to gain access to your computer.

Attackers target some programs more than other programs. The most targeted programs are normally browsers and runtime engines such as Adobe Flash™ and Java™. Recently this list has expanded to include popular PDF viewers.

There are third party utilities, which monitor your installed programs and recommend or automatically update vulnerable programs.

For a complete list, look at this books web reference at HealthyPasswords.com .

Think before you click

If you are unexpectedly prompted for something while browsing the web or reading email, do the following:

1. Stop and read the message.

2. Does it look like the result of something you were doing?
   If you are not sure, close the browser and start over again.

> *As long as you're not closing important unsaved work, aborting and starting over will not cause problems. Follow your gut instinct!*

Don't Get Hooked

One of the most common attacks is called phishing (pronounced fishing). This is where someone sends an unsolicited email hoping a user will respond. It usually looks like it is coming from some bank you never heard of asking you to update security information. On occasion, it may be from the very bank you use. A good policy is never click on any link in an email. Open the browser and navigate there on your own by typing the URL.

If you are using a system with parental controls built in, like Apple's MAC OS-X, you can create a separate account and enable parental controls to restrict the browser to only the sites you specify. Doing this is a good way to prevent phishing attacks. Using the separate account makes this feasible. If you tried this with your everyday account, you would quickly tire of adding websites to the parental controls.

Cryptic Email from Friends

Most people have received an email from someone they know entitled "Check this out" (Or something like that), but there only is a link or attachment? Don't click on the link or open the attachment. Just close the message.

If you are concerned about someone's feelings, create a new message asking if they sent you the previous email. Chances are they did not send it, and you have just alerted them that they have a virus on their machine that needs to be rectified.

Fake Virus Warnings

If you see a message on your screen saying you have a virus and it looks like it is legitimate, but when you follow removal instructions, you find they want you to buy something, do not fall for it. Get your system cleaned by a professional.

Summary

1. Clean your machine before changing your passwords.

2. Use limited rights accounts.

3. Install virus and malware protection.

4. Keep the computer patched.

5. Be careful with USB/Flash drives.

6. Don't click on email links.

Healthy Passwords

Your First Menu

Create your very own menu!

It is time to put everything learned to good use and begin making strong passwords. Do not jump in too quickly. You need a strategy. If you just start making strong passwords, you will end up frustrated waiting for emails from each site you forgot the password to.

Follow these steps to implement your plan:

1. Take inventory of the sites you use.

2. Assign risk levels to each site.

3. Determine two main ingredients and a few breads and condiments.

4. Devise variations by site based on the ingredient list you created.

5. Test out your passwords to see if your fingers like them.

6. Start changing passwords.

7. Adjust your strategy.

Step 1 - Take Inventory of the Sites You Use

You can download a worksheet from this book's website, www.HealthyPasswords.com , or you can make your own. List all the sites you use.

Site	Risk	Existing Password
BigBank.com	High	
ToolTalk.com	Low	
SocialCity.com	Medium	

For a few weeks, record your existing sites and passwords. You'll be amazed how many sites you forgot to include in your first list.

Don't start changing passwords yet. It helps to get a good idea of all the sites before you create your plan.

Step 2 - Assign Risk Levels to Each Site

To the right of each site name, assign a risk level. You can determine risk level by using the following criteria:

Highest Risk Site Characteristics

1. Bank account information:

   Banks, Retirement Accounts, Bill payment and some shopping sites using direct debit.

2. Social Security Number:

   Credit monitoring and government sites.

3. Intimate Personal Information:

   Dating Services and health care records.

4. Offsite backup services:

   They have a copy of every document on your computer or perhaps even network storage device. These sites could easily keep old tax returns, bank statements, photos, resumes, etc.

5. Online tax preparation sites.

These have your tax returns, enough
said!

High Risk Site Characteristics

1. Credit card information:
   Shopping sites that keep your credit
   card information for fast checkout.

2. Purchase history information:
   Some super web stores are the new
   general store. They know every
   household good you use and every book
   you've read.

3. Access to impersonate you:
   Sites that let you post or broadcast
   information can cause embarrassment if
   someone wants to vandalize your
   personal image.

4. Access to customer information:
   The last thing any business person
   wants to do is lose their customer
   information.

Moderate Risk Site Characteristics

1. Personal Information:
   Name, address, phone, likes and dislikes

are already more public than ever, why make it worse?

2. Family Information:
   Details about your family like names, addresses, phone numbers, ages, pictures, etc.

> *Some people don't care if others look at pictures of their family. Any information you can withhold from a predator is advantageous to you. Why take chances?*

3. Career Information:
   When we're looking for a job, we gladly give out our resumes, but when someone takes it, it may not be the picture you want to paint.

4. Photographs:
   Many sites are designed to share your photos. It's best when you can maintain control over who sees them.

Step 3 - Determine ingredients.

This is where you need to decide how complicated to get. It is better to start simple rather than be overwhelmed. Pick an easy short phrase based main ingredient. If you missed the section in Rule one on choosing a main ingredient, re-read that section.

> *If you decide to use a three character main ingredient, just be sure to add enough spice and condiments to be at least eight characters long.*
>
> *For example:*
>
> *q2!Tbm@fb*
>
> *[2nd Quarter Expiration] [Three blind mice] [at FACEBOOK]*

After using the simpler ingredients for a few months, you can re-evaluate your list to make it stronger.

Step 4 - Devise variations by site based on the ingredient list you created.

This is where the listing pays off. As you scan your listing in order, you can ensure that similar site types use similar formatting by slightly altering ingredients.

For example:

Risk Level	Site	Top Bread	Condiment	Main Ingredient	Condiment	Bottom Bread
Highest	First Bank	Fb	@	TbmShtr	!	Q1
Highest	Second Bank	Sb	@	TbmShtr	!	Q2
High	Amazon™	az	@	Shtr		A2
High	Overstock™	os	@	Shtr		A2
Moderate	Twitter™	tw	@	Tbm		A2
Moderate	Facebook™	fb	@	Tbm		A1
Low	Knitters Anonymous			Jrdjsd		
Low	Cats Best Friend			Jrdjsd		

Since you are just starting out, keeping it simple is the best way to ensure success.

Passwords within the same risk group are very similar. Some of the differences between the groups are:

1. Highest risk passwords use a two-part main ingredient. High and moderate risk sites use a one-part main ingredient.

2. Highest risk passwords include an exclamation point condiment before the expiration.

3. The AT symbol (@) is used as a site identifier suffix for all but low risk levels. The site identifier is unique for each site.

   It would be better to use a different condiment for the moderate risk sites, but it might be too difficult to remember. Again, start simple, once you feel comfortable, change it later.

4. If you're just starting with all new passwords, your expiration dates will all be the same for each site type.

   This example assumes you're

starting this in January, 2011. These will change as you log in over different times.

Expiration is the only part you really have to memorize for each site. Over time, these should all change to be slightly different. For sites you don't log into more than once a month, you may need to make a note on the back of your wallet card (we'll get to the wallet card soon) to remember some of them.

5. All the low risk sites can use your favorite junk food password. Remember these are the sites that keep nothing important and just need a login to retrieve your settings.

Step 5 – Test your passwords

Before you start changing passwords, it is important to test them out.

Open up a simple text editor and try typing each password a few times.

- Is there a special character that is difficult to type? Now is the time to adjust it.

- Is it too long? Any password with more than 10 characters seems long at first. Once your fingers begin to remember the password, it becomes easier. If you've tried it a few dozen times, and you are hitting backspace more than typing, you need to revise. Remember, it is easier to revise before you start changing them.

Step 6 - Start changing passwords.

Once you start changing passwords, you will find you have to make adjustments. Some sites restrict characteristics of your passwords.

Print a fresh copy of the password worksheet, and this time write the new password down.

Some common password restrictions are:

1. At least 8 characters.

2. At least one letter and number.

3. At least one special character.

4. Some sites don't allow any special characters, which may force you to alter your strategy. See Step 6 (next)

5. Many sites don't allow passwords
   longer than 14 characters.

Try to incorporate most of the restrictions
for the sites you use. Until you try changing
passwords, you will not know all the
restrictions you will hit. Sites have varying
opinions about the qualities a password
must have.

Step 7 – Make a wallet card

Because you are using this system, a wallet card is a good way to record your passwords without giving them away. You will not have to lose sleep worrying about losing your wallet and all your passwords.

If you keep passwords uniform by risk level, you only need to note the formula in shorthand for each risk level.

Hgst: ss at 3br1 3br2 ex Qx

Hg: ss at 3br2 Ax

Mod: ss at 3br1 Ax

Low: k2k1

You can use the back-side of the card to note exceptions.

If someone finds your wallet card, they will not have any idea what it is for. You will only need to remember how sites were classified and some of your shorthand.

Ss=Site Identifier

3br1 = Three Blind Mice (3 blind rodents part 1)

3br2 = See how they run (3 blind rodents part 2)

Ax = Annual Expiration

Qx = Quarterly Expiration

K2 = 2nd Child initials

K1 = 1st Child initials

At = @

Ex = !

Step 8 - Adjust your strategy.

If individual site restrictions ruin your plan, try to work around them. If you make your passwords meet the five common rules in Step-6, you will be safer for most sites.

When you hit one with an odd restriction, try to handle it as close to your plan as possible. For example, let us say that First Bank did not allow special characters. You could change it from fb@TbmShtr!q1 to fbATbmShtrXq1.

> *The first week you use the new passwords, your fingers may have a hard time remembering your phrases. It usually takes about ten days before they start to feel natural. If you happened to pick a series of characters you just can't seem to get used to, go back to your list and change it. Some things look great on paper, but never seem to work in practice.*

Prevention

1. Do not leave breadcrumbs.

    It is convenient to have your computer remember site passwords, but every saved password leaves a "breadcrumb" behind.

    Viruses or Trojans can test encrypted (hashed) passwords millions of times in the background without your knowledge.

    Typing passwords when you login will help you memorize them and more importantly, it will remind you when they expire and should change.

2. Keep your machine patched

    Setup your computer to receive updates and when you're told updates are ready, apply them[3].

    Updates come out regularly and patch the biggest holes, which let bad people use your machine.

---

[3] If you are logging in with a limited rights account for day-to-day activities, you may have to log in as administrator to perform system updates.

There are third-party utilities which help to manage patches. For a complete list, see HealthyPasswords.com.

3. Take extra caution with finance

Follow the advice and use special accounts or live-cds to access your finances.

Never go to a finance site from an email link. Open the browser and type the URL yourself.

4. Use quick checkout options sparingly

It is convenient to use quick checkout. Just remember that if someone gets your information, you could be inviting a shopping spree. Even though most sites will require re-validation of credit card numbers when you change shipping addresses, most will let you purchase gift cards to send to email addresses.

Ken S. Klein

> *It's easy for criminals to setup a fake email for online gift cards. Even though they can track down the person who eventually uses the cards, many unsuspecting work-at-home victims (money mules) end up getting blamed for these.*

When will passwords be obsolete?

For years, alternate authentication systems have failed to gain widespread use. Some of the alternate methods trying to replace passwords are:

Two step verification

Google™ users may sign up for a new two-step system by updating their profile. Users must provide a mobile device number when they sign up. At login, the user provides a user-name and password. If these are valid, the system then sends a text message to a predetermined Mobile device. The message contains a temporary "verification code". The user then enters the verification code in the next screen. If the code matches the one sent via text message, the user may access to their account.

This type of security system is much more robust than traditional password type systems. An attacker would have to first know your user-name and password, and then they must possess the mobile device. In all likelihood, very few people using this security will have their accounts compromised. Possible negatives are for people without unlimited text message plans, and people who don't normally keep their mobile phones with them.

Biometrics

Biometrics use hardware readers for authentication. The most common is a fingerprint reader. Many laptops now have finger print scanners built in. The problem with these systems is that they require a middle layer of software running on the device, which reads the fingerprint, looks up a password, and fills the form of the requesting website. If you use a single machine, this may be ok. If you roam between machines, you will still need to learn the passwords. Also, by keeping the passwords in a middle-layer, they leave breadcrumbs with the password information on the machine, which could be decoded.

Security Tokens

These are small key-chain devices, which are about the size of an automobile wireless remote. Some manufacturers of these products also offer software based tokens, thus eliminating the key-chain device. They have a small LCD display that shows a long number every 30 seconds.

Like the Google™ two-step verification process, the user must first enter their password. The second step is to enter the number currently displayed on the token. The number changes periodically (usually every 30-60 seconds). If everything matches up, the user may access the resources.

Large corporations most commonly use tokens for VPN access. Verisign has recently created a new token for consumers. It works on several sites now. If it becomes popular, we all may have one someday. The negative to tokens is that they only work on a limited number of sites and the device can be lost. When a device is lost, it is useless to anyone who finds it, but the user has the inconvenience of waiting for a replacement.

Until the user gets the hang of timing their login with the device, it can also prove frustrating when the time window ends right after entering the long number, but before the server receives the message.

Living Wills

If you are incapacitated, a living will helps fulfil your requests when you cannot. Including your accounts and passwords with these papers can help.

When someone takes over for you, they typically check your paper mail, but they may not know to check your email and make online payments for you. Be sure all your email accounts and online payments are included.

The last thing your family needs, is delinquency notices or bill collection agencies during an already stressful time.

We all Die

Even when we die, our passwords will not be obsolete. Social networking sites are loaded with pages of dead people haunting their friends and family members.

> *Do your executor a favor and put a copy of your password list (no shorthand) with your will.*

If you have a will, you are probably a good planner. Leave instructions in your will to close all your various accounts out. Be sure to explain expiration dates, so they may easily determine the password based on your last year, quarter or month. If you want to be nice, buy an extra copy of this book and put it with the will as well.

Summary

1. Create your site list.

2. Assign risk levels.

3. Create passwords using a common strategy.

4. Keep a list of sites and passwords somewhere away from your computer.

5. Put a copy of the list with your will.

6. If you store the list electronically or post it next to your computer, use shorthand for that copy.

Appendix A – Creating Additional User Accounts

Creating user accounts can vary greatly depending on the OS version. Following these steps will most likely not work exactly as described. Hopefully, they will be close enough to enable successful setup of additional accounts on your machines.

If you are trying to perform these steps on a work machine, please consult your local IT department before attempting to setup additional accounts. You may not be able to do this on a company owned machine.

> *If your system currently is configured for auto-login, be sure you know the password to your main account before you change anything. If you turn off auto-login and then log out, you may not be able to get back into your system. In most cases, the account you are currently using to auto login, will not have a password.*

Microsoft Windows™

There are several different versions of Microsoft
Windows that you could be running. The
necessary steps vary based upon the version.
Some older versions do not offer accounts.

Managing Accounts

1. Click on the start menu. The start menu is
   normally in the lower left hand corner of
   your screen.

2. Find "My Computer" listed in the start menu.

3. Right Click on "My Computer".

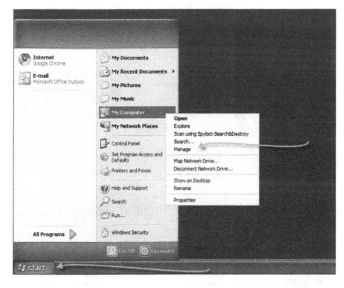

4. Select "Manage"

5. The computer management applet will appear.

Creating a new Account

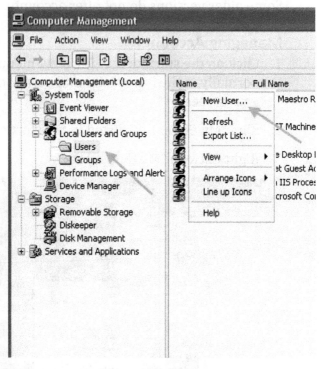

1. In the left-hand pane, expand "Local Users and Groups".

2. Click once on users.

3. A listing of currently configured accounts will appear in the right hand pane.

4. Right click in the right hand pane.

5. Select "New User..." from the right click menu.

Configuring the New Account

The new user applet will appear.

1. Create a user name.

   This example creates an account for the kids
   to use. Depending on the age of your kids,
   you may want individual accounts for them.
   A good general rule is to create their own
   account when they start sending email.

2. Create a temporary password for them.

   When they first login it will ask them for a new one. Use this as a learning experience to teach your children about passwords. If you prefer to set the password yourself, uncheck the "User must change password at next logon" option.

3. Select "Create" to create the account.

4. Select close to close the new user dialog.

   The list will now display the new username.

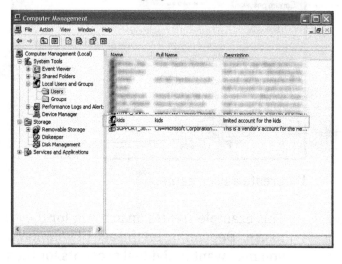

5. Double Click on the newly created account.

    The "Account Name" Properties dialog will appear.

6. Select the "Member Of" tab.

   The member of tab will receive focus.

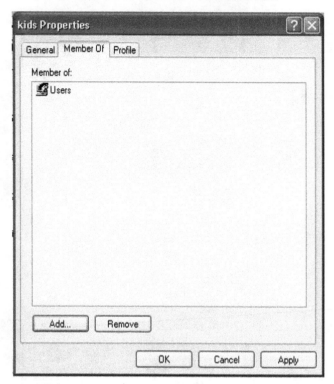

Limiting Rights

If the user account created requires email, just leave the default "Users" group as the only member group.

If the user does not need email (they may use webmail), you can further restrict the account by removing the users group and adding the guests group. This will limit the user to the least rights possible without using something called policies, which provide robust customization by user.

1. From the member of tab, click Add.

The Select Groups dialog will appear.

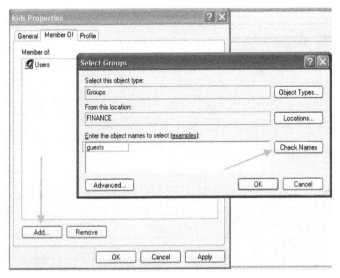

2. In the "Enter the object names to select dialog, type "guests"

3. Select "Check Names" the guests text you entered will change to computername\guests.

4. Select OK.

The Member of tab will return to focus with "Guests" added to the list.

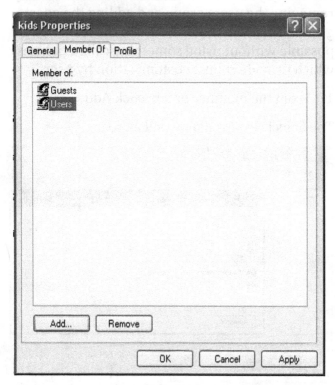

5. Single click on Users once then click remove.

   The member of tab will return to focus with only "Guests" in the list.

6. Select OK to close the user properties dialog.

Test the new Account

To test the newly created account, logoff the current account.

1. Select "Log off" from the start menu.

2. If "log off" is not available, select "windows security" then logoff.

3. At the Welcome to Windows screen, Hold down CTRL+ALT then press and release DEL.

4. Change the user name to the username you just created and type in the initial password you set then select OK.

5. The first time you login, the change password message may display. This will only occur if the "User Must Change Password at Next Login" option was selected (See page 120)

6. Press OK to return to the login screen.

7. Put in the new password twice then select ok.

A message will display that the password has changed.

8. Select OK.

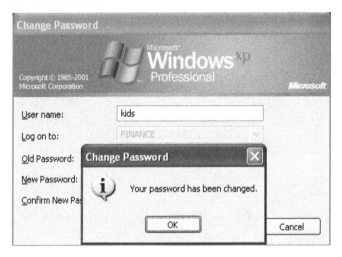

The first login will be slower than normal while the new account is setup.

Test the functions you require under this account.

If you are just using a web browser, no additional setup may be required. If you use other programs, you may find they do not function correctly under the new account. Getting other programs to run properly under limited rights accounts is a more advanced top, and you may need help from a professional.

Remember that you can login as your old account and nothing will have changed there.

Apple OS-X™

There are many versions of OS-X. This will document the settings on OS-X 10.4 (Tiger). The latest version, leopard, is very similar.

Managing accounts

1. Run system preferences from the Dock.

Note: Different versions of OS-X may use different icons for "System Preferences" Hover over the icon to find the appropriate one.

2. Select "Accounts" under system.

3. Unlock the little padlock icon in the lower left to enable changes then click on + to add.

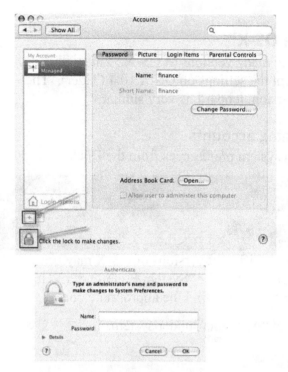

4. If prompted to enter an administrator's username and password, do so. Enter the admin username and password.

5. The new user dialog will appear. Enter a username, a short name, and password.

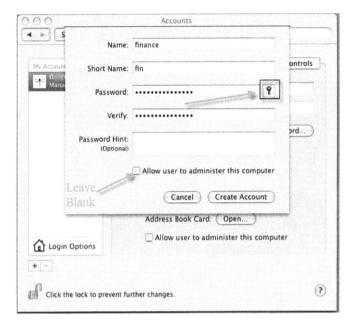

In the above screenshot, the little key icon to the right of the password was clicked. This displays the password assistant. This utility is an example of a password checker. Play with this a bit. As you type the password, tips will appear.

6. To create the account, select "create account".

7. If you are running a newer version of OS-X, you may see additional roles available. This screenshot is from Snow Leopard.

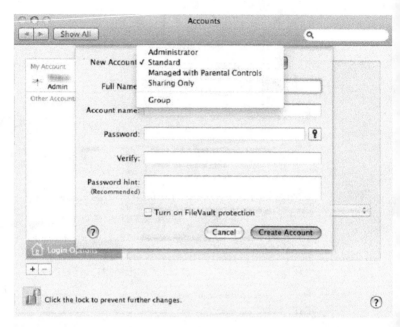

Notice you can select various roles.

Parental Controls for Finance

Later versions of OS-X include parental controls.
Use these to provide an additional layer of security
for your financial account. These controls are set to
disallow all sites except those explicitly added by an
admin. Restricting access to the few financial sites
required, prevents tricking a user into going to the
wrong site by a phishing email or other means.

At a minimum, safari should be restricted.

1. From the accounts system configuration application, select the parental controls tab. Make sure the finance account is the one selected in the left hand column. You may have to unlock the page by entering an admin user as was done in step 3 before.

2. The parental controls tab will display. Check the safari tab.

3. Apply the changes by clicking on the padlock in the lower left corner.

4. Run Safari and enter your financial institution's web address (URL) in the Safari address bar. The page will be blocked.

5. Click Add Website. You will be prompted to enter an admin username and password. Enter the admin credentials.

6. Site access is granted upon entering the admin ID/Password and a bookmark dialog will appear. If you wish to add the bookmark, do so.

7. Repeat this step for each financial site. You may have to add additional entries for the same financial institution depending upon their internet address naming conventions.

Appendix B – WiFi™

WiFi™ is not a manufacturer or brand of equipment. The WiFi alliance is a non-profit organization that sets wireless standards. For equipment to earn their label, it must meet their specifications and pass a testing process similar to the United States' UL or the European Union's CE programs.

If your network equipment has the WiFi™ label and was manufactured after March 2006, it will offer an encryption called WPA-2. If your device offers WPA-2, use it. If it does not, buy a new device and configure it to use WPA-2.

Configuration of Home WiFi™ varies greatly amongst manufacturers. Most newer WIFI equipment will offer at least five options for security:

SSID Broadcast

The SSID is the name of the network. Hiding the name does not change much in terms of security. Hiding this won't slow down the geek next door, but it will hinder you every time a guest needs to use your network or you get a new device.

MAC Address Filtering

MAC address filtering will prevent a casual user from getting onto your network, but like hiding SSID, the geek next door will quickly get around this. Also, if you have people visit your house and access your wireless network, maintaining this type of feature will be very cumbersome.

WEP

This is the oldest type of wireless encryption. There are many widely available programs which will quickly break WEP encryption, so like the previous settings, the geek next door may need an extra few minutes to break WEP.

WPA

This was meant to be an interim solution between WEP and WPA/2. WPA is more secure than WEP, but our geek next door can still break this.

WPA/2

Currently, this is the most secure form of wireless encryption available in home networking equipment. The key to making this secure is to use a strong wireless password. If you're really paranoid, you can go up to 63 characters for your password. A casual home user should have a password no less than 10 characters. If you live in a large apartment complex in Silicon Valley, or on a technical college campus, you may want to double that length.

Glossary

ACCOUNT

The files, folders, network and local privileges for a USERID or USERNAME assigned on the system.

ACRONYM

A word formed from the initial letters of a name.

AUTHENTICATION

Security measure designed to protect a communications system against fraudulent transmissions and establish the authenticity of a message.

BANDWIDTH

The amount of data that can be passed along a communications channel in a given period of time.

BIOMETRICS

The measurement of physical characteristics, such as fingerprints, DNA, or retinal patterns, for use in verifying the identity of individuals.

CELLULAR CARD

A wireless network adapter for a laptop, PDA or cellphone that provides cellular data transmission.

CHARACTER SUBSTITION

Using symbols in place of letters. For example PASSWORD could be P@$$W0RD.

CRACKING PROGRAMS

Programs which use various methods to rapidly determine the password for a given user.

DICTIONARY WORD

Any word which can be found in a common dictionary including: reversed words, acronyms, and common people, places and things, profanity, pop-culture expressions, or any of the previous using character substitions.

ENCRYPTION

A procedure that renders the contents of a computer message or file unintelligible to anyone not authorized to read it.

FISHING

See Phishing.

FLASH DRIVE

See USB Drive.

HTTPS

HTTPS stands for HyperText Transport Protocol Secure. This is normally used for on-line banking and screens where you enter your password. You can tell if you are on an encrypted connection by looking at the the address bar in your browser. The URL will begin with HTTPS and in many browsers there will be a special icon. If you click that icon, you can usually view the sites certificate.

HASH

Encoding algorithms used to encrypt character streams.

LINUX

A Nonproprietary operating system for computers.

NETWORK ATTACHED STORAGE (NAS)

A stand-alone hard drive that is connected to a network and is always on enabling users to store and retrieve files.

NON-WRITABLE OS

> An operating system that can run programs but cannot be altered. Every time the machine restarts, the operating system starts over not remembering any past session settings.

OFFSITE BACKUP

> The act of copying files to a service which stores files in another location. These are used for disaster recovery.

OPERATING SYSTEM

> Software that organizes and manages resources of system, communicates with peripherals, interacts with users, handles files, and accesses software.

PHISHING

> Internet scam designed to trick the recipient into revealing credit card, passwords, social security numbers and other personal information to individuals who intend to use them for fraudulent purposes.

ROUTER

> A device in a network that handles message transfers between computers (your home/office and the internet).

SOCIAL NETWORKING

> Social networking is a term used to describe websites where people can share information and collaborate with others about similar interests.

THIRD PARTY SOFTWARE

> Software designed and sold by a different company than the operating system vendor.

TROJANS

> A malicious program which enters a users system posing as something helpful.

USB DRIVE

> A portable data storage device that receives power from the USB port of a computer.

USER ID

> The credential used by a person to access a computer account.

VIRTUAL MACHINE

> A software program that emulates a hardware system.

VIRUS

A malicious program which enters a users system without their knowledge or approval.

WIFI™

A trademark for the certification of products that meet certain standards for transmitting data over wireless networks.

Index

C

D

E

F

M

N

O

P

U

V

W

www.ingramcontent.com/pod-product-compliance
Lightning Source LLC
Chambersburg PA
CBHW071204050326
40689CB00011B/2241

*9 780615 456850 *